PRESIDENTIAL LIBRARIES™

RONALD REAGAN
PRESIDENTIAL LIBRARY

Amy Margaret

The Rosen Publishing Group's
PowerKids Press™

New York

For Matthew and Blake

Acknowledgement: The author would like to thank Margaret Ahlberg for her invaluable assistance on this project. Thank you also to the Ronald Reagan Presidential Library for their support and review of this book.

Published in 2004 by The Rosen Publishing Group, Inc.
29 East 21st Street, New York, NY 10010

First Edition

Editor: Joanne Riethoff
Book Design: Maria E. Melendez

Photo credits: All photos courtesy of the Ronald Reagan Library except p. 17 (top) © AP/Wide World Photos.

Margaret, Amy.
Ronald Reagan Presidential Library / Amy Margaret.— 1st ed.
    v. cm. — (Presidential libraries)
Includes bibliographical references and index.
Contents: A visit to the library and museum — The president as a child — Ronald Reagan, the actor — The road to the presidency — Presidential highlights — The First Lady — Family man — After the White House — Museum and library exhibits — Did you know? — Glossary.
ISBN 0-8239-6272-5 (lib. bdg.)
1. Ronald Reagan Presidential Library—Juvenile literature. 2. Reagan, Ronald—Archives—Juvenile literature. 3. Presidents—United States—Archives—Juvenile literature. 4. Reagan, Ronald—Museums—California—Simi Valley—Juvenile literature. 5. Reagan, Ronald—Juvenile literature. 6. Presidents—United States—Biography—Juvenile literature. [1. Ronald Reagan Presidential Library. 2. Reagan, Ronald. 3. Presidents.] I. Title.
E838.5 .R439 M37 2003
973.927'092—dc21

2001007978

Manufactured in the United States of America

CONTENTS

A VISIT TO THE LIBRARY AND MUSEUM

The Ronald Reagan Presidential Library opened in 1991, in Simi Valley, California. The building was designed in a style similar to that of the **Spanish missions** of California. Spanish tile, **adobe** tile, and redwood are used throughout the structure. The library grounds feature plants and trees native to California.

The library also houses a museum and sits on about 100 acres (40 ha) of land in Simi Valley, picked out by Reagan himself. Presidential libraries are run by the **National Archives and Records Administration** (NARA), so that the public can learn about what certain presidents have done in their lives.

The Ronald Reagan Presidential Library is located in Simi Valley, California. In the 1950s, many Hollywood movies and television programs were made in Simi Valley. Reagan was once an actor in Hollywood. He appeared in several movies.

Above: Reagan starred in this war movie that came out in 1957 with his wife Nancy.

The Ronald Reagan Presidential Library is the largest of all the presidential libraries and museums. It holds almost 55 million pages of government records and more than 1.5 million photographs.

THE PRESIDENT AS A CHILD

Ronald had one brother, Neil, who was older and was nicknamed Moon. This picture of Ronald (right) with his brother (left) was taken in 1912.

Ronald Reagan was born on February 6, 1911, in Tampico, Illinois. His father, Jack Reagan, thought the baby looked like a Dutchman, so Ronald was nicknamed Dutch. His mother, Nelle, sewed to earn extra money. Ronald's father was a salesman. While Jack was on the road, Ronald would take on the role of his father.

In the fall of 1928, Ronald attended Eureka College in Eureka, Illinois. In his first year at college, he saw a play performed by **professional** actors. He knew then that he wanted to be an actor. At the presidential library museum, Ronald's college class ring, **varsity letter** sweater, and yearbook are on **exhibit**.

This is a family picture taken in Illinois in 1915. Left to right: Jack, Neil, four-year-old Ronald, and Nelle.

Ronald was an outstanding swimmer. At age 15, Ronald worked as a lifeguard at a local park. In his six summers working there, Ronald saved 77 people. During this time, he began to show his leadership abilities. This picture was taken during the summer of 1927 in Lowell Park, in Dixon, Illinois.

RONALD REAGAN, THE ACTOR

When Reagan was attending Eureka College, he got a job as a sports announcer for a radio station in Iowa, which he continued after college. At the museum, you can see a copy of the microphone he used at the radio station during the mid-1930s. The picture above shows Reagan at WHO radio station in Des Moines, Iowa.

While at Eureka College, Ronald Reagan studied **economics**. He graduated in June 1932.

In 1937, Reagan traveled to Los Angeles doing work for a radio station. Reagan eventually signed a seven-year contract with Warner Bros. Studio, one of the biggest studios in Hollywood. He made more than 50 low-cost movies.

In 1941, the United States joined World War II. Reagan went in for his medical check to become a soldier, but his eyesight was not strong enough for him to be sent to the battlefields. Reagan wanted to be involved, so he used his film knowledge to help create training films that prepared soldiers for fighting.

After the war ended in 1945, Reagan became the president of the Screen Actors Guild (SAG). This group protected the wages and the working hours of actors. Left: Reagan is shown here on the set of GE Theater during the 1950s.

One wall in the museum has information about Reagan's acting career. It shows many photographs and posters from the movies in which he acted.

FAMILY MAN

Reagan's love for Nancy will never be forgotten because of the letters he wrote to her throughout their life together. In 2000, the letters were put together in a book called *I Love You, Ronnie*. Above: *Ronald Reagan and Nancy Davis were married on March 4, 1952. Here they are standing in front of their wedding cake.*

Ronald Reagan had four children. Reagan and his first wife, actress Jane Wyman, had a daughter, Maureen, in 1941 and adopted Michael in 1945. After he divorced Jane, Reagan married Nancy Davis in 1952. They had Patti that year and Ronald Jr. in 1958.

The Reagan children have had various jobs, from dancing for the Joffrey Ballet to writing to acting. Reagan's oldest daughter, Maureen, died in 2001 from skin **cancer**.

Ronald and Nancy Reagan had a very special relationship. Ronald wrote Nancy love letters throughout their lives. The original letters are housed at the Ronald Reagan Presidential Library.

This is a family picture taken in the 1970s in Pacific Palisades, California. Left to Right: *Patti, Nancy, Ronald, Michael, Maureen, and Ron.*

THE FIRST LADY

At the White House, Nancy Reagan worked to educate kids on the dangers of drug abuse. Her program was called Just Say No. It urged children to say no when asked to try drugs. Here Nancy is pictured at a Just Say No rally in Los Angeles, California, on May 11, 1987.

Nancy Reagan was born Anne Frances Robbins on July 6, 1921. She was nicknamed Nancy. Her parents divorced, and her mother, Edith, remarried several years later. Edith's new husband, Dr. Loyal Davis, adopted Nancy and she became Nancy Davis.

Nancy went to Hollywood to act and met Ronald Reagan. They married on March 4, 1952.

When Ronald became **governor** of California in 1967, Nancy learned about the Foster Grandparent Program (FGP). This program allows older people to get involved with children who need special attention. She supported FGP then and as First Lady, too.

Nancy was very involved in world events, as were First Ladies before her. Here she is shown visiting the earthquake-damaged areas of Mexico City, Mexico. This photograph was taken on September 23, 1985.

In this photograph, Nancy is conducting the National Symphony in Washington, D.C. This photograph was taken on March 27, 1987.

THE ROAD TO THE PRESIDENCY

Ronald and Nancy Reagan are shown above boarding LeaderShip 80, in 1980. They are on their way to campaign for the presidency. For the 1980 election, Reagan used slogans such as "I'm a Democrat for Reagan" and "Regain Reason with Reagan." You can see these slogans on bumper stickers and buttons at the museum.

Throughout his life, Reagan considered himself a **Democrat**, like his father. After the war, Reagan became more **conservative**. In 1952, he supported Dwight D. Eisenhower, a **Republican**, for president. In 1962, Reagan joined the Republican party.

Reagan ran for governor of California in 1966. In 1974, he decided to run for president. Reagan had to be **nominated** by the Republican party. In 1976, he ran against President Gerald Ford, who won that year.

Reagan refused to give up. A video at the museum shows Reagan saying on November 13, 1979, that he will run for president again. In 1980, he won.

When Reagan was elected governor in 1966, he won by a million votes. Here Reagan is shown being sworn in as governor of California as his young son Ron watches. This photograph was taken in January 1967, in Sacramento, California.

When Reagan won the presidency in 1980, he was 71 years old, the oldest president so far. In this picture the Reagans are shown in the 1981 Inaugural Parade on January 20, 1981, in Washington, D.C.

REAGANOMICS

Only 10 weeks after Reagan moved into the White House, someone tried to kill him. He was rushed into surgery to remove the bullet that had lodged near his heart. At the museum, you can see Reagan's X ray, showing the bullet. On display there is also a bulletproof vest, one of many sent to him after the attack. This picture was taken on March 30, 1981, at the Washington Hilton hotel just minutes before Reagan was shot.

Reagan had a plan known as Reaganomics. It included balancing government expenses and increasing both the spending for the country's defense and the power of each citizen. When Reagan left the White House, the nation had experienced six years of economic growth, the longest recorded period of growth during peacetime.

During Reagan's second term, he met with the general secretary of the Soviet Union, Mikhail Gorbachev. Their meetings resulted in the first agreement to reduce the number of **nuclear weapons**. This **treaty** was called the Intermediate-Range Nuclear Forces (INF) Treaty, and the men signed it in December 1987.

Top: *President Reagan (second from the right) and Soviet leader Mikhail Gorbachev (second from the left) sign the Intermediate-Range Nuclear Forces Treaty and other documents during a ceremony in the White House East Room. This photograph was taken on December 8, 1987. This treaty got rid of all the ground-launched, medium-range missiles in both nations. This was the first real cut in either nation's store of weapons. There is an 11-minute video showing this event at the museum in one of its theaters. Bottom: An example of the kind of missile they were talking about is shown at the museum, too.*

GIFTS FIT FOR A PRESIDENT

The Ronald Reagan Presidential Library is full of gifts the Reagans received while in the White House. One gift on exhibit is a chunk of coral with silver coins **embedded** into it, given by the president of the Dominican Republic. The coins are from a Spanish ship that sank in 1690. The queen of Thailand gave Reagan an ivory elephant covered with gold. It has precious jewels set in it.

There is also a case at the museum devoted to gifts, known as White House gifts, from Americans. Many of them are handmade. They include a quilt, a needlepoint clock, and a hooked rug. All these gifts have a picture of the White House in the artwork.

This picture is of Reagan making a toast to Australian prime minister Malcolm Fraser at a state dinner on June 30, 1981, in the White House. At these dinners, national leaders would meet and talk about their countries' issues. It is at meetings and dinners like these that gifts are exchanged. These gifts represent each country's way of life.

One of the largest gifts given to Reagan is outside on the deck overlooking Simi Valley. It is a 6,000-pound (2,722-kg) piece of the Berlin Wall, given to Reagan by the Berlin Wall Commemorative Group. The Berlin Wall, which divided the city of Berlin for almost 30 years, was torn down at the end of Reagan's presidency in 1989. The wall was taken apart as a sign that the cold war had ended. The cold war was a time in U.S. history when the Soviet Union and the United States competed for power. The cold war ended in large part because of the talks between Reagan and Gorbachev.

LIFE AFTER THE WHITE HOUSE

Three months after doctors found out that Reagan had Alzheimer's disease, Reagan wrote a letter to the American people. He wrote, "At the moment I feel just fine. I intend to live the remainder of the years God gives me on this earth doing the things I have always done." Shown above is a picture of the museum display about Reagan's disease.

After eight years in the White House, Ronald and Nancy Reagan moved to a home in Bel Air, in Los Angeles. They split their time between the Bel Air home and their ranch, Rancho del Cielo, outside of Santa Barbara. Many items from the ranch are exhibited at the museum. The couple wrote books on their lives and traveled with friends to places such as Alaska.

In August 1994, doctors found the beginnings of **Alzheimer's disease** in Reagan. As would any true leader, he announced his illness to the public that year. By 1997, Reagan ended all public appearances. Nancy still attends important functions when she can.

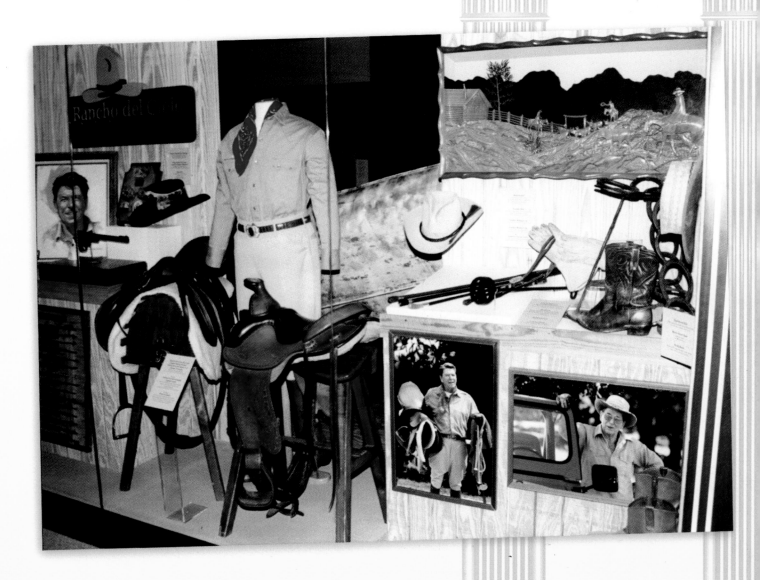

The Reagans spend much of their time at their ranch, Rancho del Cielo. An exhibit at the museum displays items, such as boots, hats, and gloves, used by the Reagans at the ranch.

DID YOU KNOW?

Here are some fun facts to share with your friends about the fortieth president of the United States:

In 1940, Ronald Reagan was voted Most Nearly Perfect Male Figure by the Division of Fine Arts at the University of Southern California.

Ronald Reagan's favorite comic strip is *Peanuts*, by Charles Schulz.

In March 2001, an aircraft carrier was named for Ronald Reagan. It is called the USS *Ronald Reagan*.

Reagan's favorite flavor of Jelly Belly jellybean is coconut.

The Reagans had two dogs living with them in the White House. They were named Lucky and Rex.

Air Force One, *the official presidential plane used by presidents Carter, Ford, Nixon, Reagan, Bush, and Clinton, was retired in September 2001. President George W. Bush uses this plane as a backup to his presidential plane. Air Force One will be housed at the Ronald Reagan Presidential Library in the spring of 2004.*

GLOSSARY

adobe (uh-DOH-bee) Brick made from dried mud and straw.

Alzheimer's disease (AHLTS-hy-merz dih-ZEEZ) An illness that causes mental problems, such as extreme forgetfulness.

cancer (KAN-ser) An illness in which cells keep growing but do not work properly.

conservative (kun-SER-vuh-tiv) Following traditional styles.

Democrat (DEH-muh-krat) A person who belongs to the Democratic party, one of the two major political parties in the United States.

economics (eh-kuh-NAH-miks) The study of production, supply, and demand of goods.

embedded (im-BED-ed) Surrounded closely.

exhibit (ig-ZIH-bit) Objects or pictures set out for people to see.

governor (GUH-vuh-nur) An official elected as head of a state.

National Archives and Records Administration (NA-shuh-nul AR-kyvz AND REH-kurdz ad-mih-nih-STRAY-shun) The group in the U.S. government that runs the 10 presidential libraries.

nominated (NAH-mih-nayt-ed) Chosen to run for political office.

nuclear weapons (NOO-klee-ur WEH-punz) Weapons that are very destructive, used during wars.

professional (proh-FEH-shuh-nul) A person who works at a job and is paid for it.

Republican (rih-PUH-blih-kuhn) A person belonging to the Republican party, one of the two major political parties in the United States.

Spanish missions (SPA-nish MIH-shunz) Religious centers set up by Spanish people in California to convert Native Americans to Christianity.

treaty (TREE-tee) A formal agreement, signed and agreed upon by each party.

varsity letter (VAR-sih-tee LEH-ter) A letter that shows an accomplishment made in a school, usually in sports.

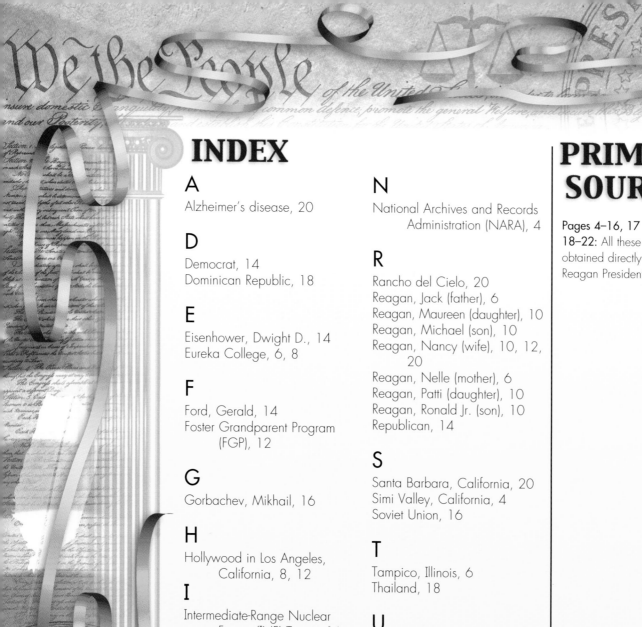

INDEX

PRIMARY SOURCES

Pages 4–16, 17 (bottom),
18–22: All these pictures were
obtained directly from the Ronald
Reagan Presidential Library.

WEB SITES

Due to the changing nature of Internet links, PowerKids Press has developed an online list of Web sites related to the subject of this book. This site is updated regularly. Please use this link to access the list:
www.powerkidslinks.com/pl/ronrlm/